Treasures of the Rainforest

An Introduction to the Endangered Forest Birds of Hawai'i

by Merryl J. Mulroney

for The Peregrine Fund

The Peregrine Fund
Hawaiian Endangered Bird Conservation Program
P.O. Box 39
Volcano, HI 96785

TREASURES OF THE RAINFOREST

An Introduction to the Endangered
Forest Birds of Hawai'i

by Merryl J. Mulroney

Published by The Peregrine Fund
Cyndi Kuehler, Alan Lieberman
Hawaiian Endangered Bird Conservation Program.

Publisher's Cataloging-in-Publication
(Provided by Quality Books, Inc.)

Mulroney, Merryl J.
    Treasures of the Rainforest: an introduction to the
endangered forest birds of Hawai'i/by Merryl J. Mulroney.
  — 1st ed.
  p.cm.
    SUMMARY: An introduction to Hawai'i's endangered forest birds,
their history, habitats, and behavior, with suggested ways children
can assist in conservation efforts.
    LCCN: 98-96888
    ISBN: 0-9669569-0-7

    1. Rain forest birds — Hawai'i — Juvenile literature.
    2. Endangered species — Juvenile literature. I. Title

QL684.H3M85 1999   598'.09969
                                   QBI199-100

Acknowledgements

The Peregrine Fund gratefully acknowledges
the following individuals and organizations
whose contributions and support have
allowed the publication of this book.

Photography: Special thanks to photographer
Jack Jeffrey, for contributing his talents and
expertise and providing many of the images.
Thanks also to Jim Denny, Linda DiSante,
Cyndi Kuehler and Joseph Kuhn.

Illustrations: Bishop Museum Archives,
Michael Furuya, Gwendolyn O'Connor, H.
Douglas Pratt and Terry Sedgwick.

Professional Support: The Peregrine Fund
staff (Keauhou Bird Conservation Center, Maui
Bird Conservation Center, World Center for
Birds of Prey); U.S. Fish and Wildlife Service,
Pacific Islands Ecoregion; Division of Forestry
and Wildlife, Hawai'i Department of Land and
Natural Resources; Biological Resources
Division of the U.S. Geological Survey; and the
Zoological Society of San Diego.

Cover photo: 'I'iwi by Jack Jeffrey.
Cover and book design by Eric Poulsen, Redbeard Graphics
Printed in U.S.A.

To Carmen and Jack Kuehler,
whose generosity made this book possible,
and to the children of Hawai'i.

CONTENTS

Wonders of the World

O n the islands of Hawai'i, rare birds dart through the canopy or forage in the lower levels of the forest. The forest birds build their nests on sheer cliff faces, in lava tubes, hollow trees or protective brush. Many birds feed on the flowers and seeds of native plants, while others poke around for insects, or drink the nectar of the brightly colored forest flowers. Found only on the islands of Hawai'i, these unique species of birds are global treasures. They exist nowhere else on earth.

For millions of years, Hawai'i was no more than a chain of bare volcanoes rising from the ocean floor. One by one, seeds, insects, snails and birds from faraway lands were carried to the islands by wind and sea. Gradually, these new life forms made their homes on Hawai'i. Today's forest birds are the descendants of these first settlers.

The closest land is more than 2,000 miles from Hawai'i, so only the strongest birds survived the journey. They came from as far away as South America and Australia. Scientists believe there were as few as thirty original bird species represented on Hawai'i. The birds helped spread seeds and pollinate plants that eventually grew into lush forests.

Changing Times

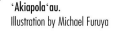

'Akiapola'au.
Illustration by Michael Furuya

In order to survive, the birds had to find new places to live and new foods to eat, so they began to change. Some developed sharp bills for cracking open seeds or ripping away bark to uncover insects. Others developed long, curved bills for feeding on nectar from trumpet-shaped flowers. Some birds changed in shape and color. Some changed their songs. With each gradual change the birds became better equipped to live in their new habitats. The changes that occurred in the birds of Hawai'i are some of the most exciting examples of evolution in the world.

When the birds first came to the islands, they left behind the diseases and natural enemies of their homelands. More than 100 new bird species had developed in Hawai'i by the time the first people arrived. Once people came to Hawai'i, the environment began to change. Today, the forest birds must fight to find safe places to live and food to eat. Many native birds are already extinct, and many more are endangered. If these birds disappear from Hawai'i, they will be gone from the earth forever.

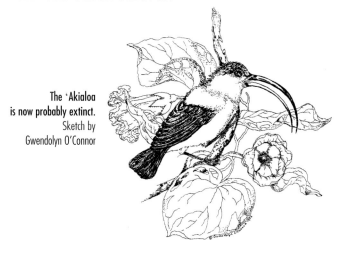

The 'Akialoa
is now probably extinct.
Sketch by
Gwendolyn O'Connor

Forces of Nature

H awai'i is famous for its mild climate, spectacular scenery and dense, tropical forests. Yet the island chain has a range of climates and habitats as varied as a large continent. Almost every ecosystem in the world is represented on this small group of islands. Each ecosystem has its own families of plants and animals and its own climate, or natural community. The plants and animals work together to help the community survive. There are more than 150 eco-systems on Hawai'i, ranging from sunny coastal grasslands to snow-covered alpine deserts. Dense rainforests cloak volcanoes clouded in heavy mist, while the windswept sides of these towering mountains

Hawai'i

Ni'ihau

Kaua'i

Alaka'i Swamp

Honolulu

O'ahu

Moloka'i

Lana'i

Kaho'olawe

Maui

Pacific Ocean

Hawai'i

Mauna Kea

Hilo

Haleakala Crater
National Park

Hawai'i Volcanoe
National Park

Long Distance Travel

The first birds were carried to Hawai'i by wind and water. The birds came from as far away as Australia and South America. If you wanted to make that trip today, you would spend over 12 hours on a plane that traveled more than 500 miles per hour. That's time for two movies, three meals, and a good long nap; and you'd still be tired when you arrived.

Mauna Kea is the highest point in Hawai'i, rising to 13,769 feet above sea level. If we measured from its base on the ocean floor, the peak would be at 33,476 feet. *The Guiness Book of World Records* believes that would make Mauna Kea the tallest mountain in the world.

give way to drier scrublands. Plants force their way through crevices in the rocky plains of lava that once spewed from volcanoes. Waterfalls tumble hundreds of feet into green valleys.

A Giant Umbrella

Hawai'i has the only tropical rainforest in the United States. The rainforests of the earth offer important shelter and resources. Modern medicines for diseases such as leukemia and malaria have been developed from plants and organisms of the forests. By studying the plants, scientists are able to find new ways to grow better crops and control diseases and pests. Rain filtered through the forests gives Hawai'i all the fresh water it needs for everyday living, business, farming and industry. The trees take in carbon dioxide and give off oxygen, helping to clean the air that we breathe and fight pollution.

More than half of

Did you know?

The mountain peak of Pu'u Kukui on Maui, has more than 400 inches of rain each year. That's more than an inch every day.

Try this!

Find a glass container and mark off one inch from the bottom. (Use a permanent marker so it doesn't wash away.) Next time it rains, place the glass jar outside and see how long it takes to fill to the one inch line.

Hawai'i's rainforest has been destroyed. Many birds continue to survive by living high in the mountains. There they find food and protection in the uppermost layer of the forest called the canopy, in the low bushes and ferns of the understory, or in the decaying vegetation on the forest floor. In higher areas of the mountains the birds depend on the koa and 'ohi'a forests. The forests, in turn, depend on them.

Imagine ...

Your school is an ecosystem. The fourth grade classroom is suddenly torn down and the fourth graders have to go to another school. They like their new school and decide not to come back, so next year there is no fifth grade, and the following year there are no students for sixth grade. Before long, no students want to attend the school because they know they will have to leave at third grade. Teachers go elsewhere to find work, buildings are not used and cared for properly. The school closes down.

The same thing happens with an ecosystem. Anytime it is altered, by cutting down plants or bringing in new ones, by adding buildings or introducing animals that change the land, everything and everyone in that ecosystem is affected. The natural community falls apart.

Birds are an important part of forest ecosystems. When plants are destroyed, the birds lose their means of food and shelter, and without the birds to spread the seeds, pollinate the flowers, and control the insects, more plants will not grow. Since humans arrived in Hawai'i less than 1600 years ago, more than fifty percent of the landscape has changed. Thousands of birds have not survived these changes.

The temple of an early king. Original drawing by Louis Choris, 1822. Bishop Museum

Humans Bring Change

The birds had the islands to themselves until the first Polynesian settlers arrived on the Big Island, around 400 A.D. These settlers began to clear the forest, planting crops of taro, breadfruit and sugar cane which thrived in the mild climate and rich soil. They brought chickens and small pigs to the islands, and rats which probably hid on their canoes. The Polynesians celebrated their connection to nature. The islands' plants and birds became an important part of their cultural heritage.

At first, the birds had no fear of people. The Polynesians began to hunt them for food, and use their feathers for decoration, clothing and in ceremonies. In 1778 Captain Cook, an English explorer, reached Hawai'i. By that time, at least thirty-five species of birds had already become extinct.

W ord of the beautiful islands spread quickly and before long, ship-loads of European settlers arrived in Hawai'i. The new settlers brought sheep, cattle, pigs and goats. They also brought fleas and lice. Whalers brought mosquitoes. In 200 years, these new settlers changed the islands more than the Polynesians had done in 1300 years. They destroyed natural vegetation to build homes and grow crops. Newly arrived plants and animals began to invade the islands. Many of the forest birds' habitats disappeared

Illustrations above and left, courtesy of Bishop Museum

and the birds became extinct.

Tourism, large scale agriculture, and uncontrolled animal pests continue to change Hawai'i. The fragile ecosystem which supports Hawai'i's remaining native inhabitants is in danger. Now seventy-four percent of forest birds are extinct or endangered.

An 'Apapane is attacked by a mosquito. Photo by Jack Jeffrey

Alien Invasions

New animals, plants, and pests harm habitats of the unique forest birds. Wild pigs roam freely, turning the forest floor into mud wallows, uprooting trees; and destroying young shoots and plants. Goats, cows and sheep eat native vegetation and trample the hillsides bare. Mongoose and rats attack young birds and eat their eggs. Mosquitoes spread avian malaria, a disease which kills the birds. Birds brought from other parts of the world spread avian pox, similar to our chicken pox, among the native birds which have no resistance to the disease.

Introduced plants also threaten the birds' habitats. Plants, such as banana poka and ginger, grow wild on the islands and strangle native plants. Once considered beautiful, many of these plants began to grow like weeds. They no longer suffered the diseases and pests which controlled them in their homelands. The plants soon took over much of the native forests.

Photo by Jack Jeffrey

Fearless Ferals

nimals kept in captivity as food or pets are domesticated. They rely on humans for food and shelter. Once these animals are abandoned or set free they must find a way to survive. They hunt for food in the wild, and become more aggressive. These feral animals, including sheep, pigs, goats and cats, destroy native vegetation or prey on the birds and their eggs.

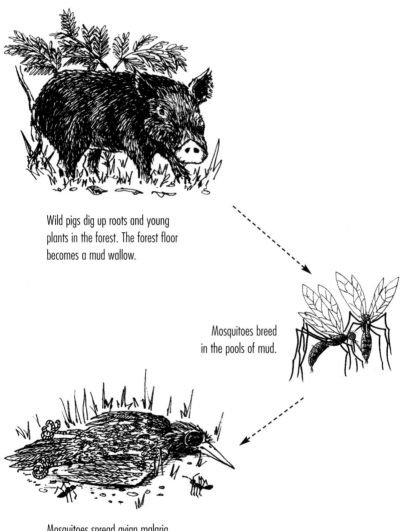

Wild pigs dig up roots and young plants in the forest. The forest floor becomes a mud wallow.

Mosquitoes breed in the pools of mud.

Mosquitoes spread avian malaria which kills many of the birds.

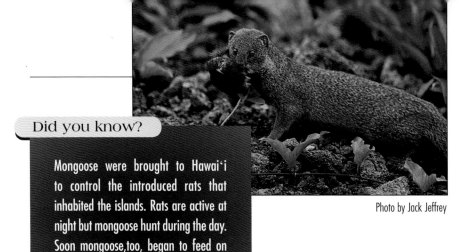

Photo by Jack Jeffrey

Cultural Traditions

Although alien animals and plants are a danger to the forest birds, some of these so-called pests have become part of Hawaiian culture. Pigs are hunted as food, especially for celebrations. Many kinds of flowers and plants are collected for decoration and ceremonial clothing. Canoes are carved from native trees, and plants are used for medicine. The chants, songs and dances of the Hawaiian people are strongly linked to nature and are important traditions, connecting the people and preserving their history. The forest birds are part of that tradition.

As people learn more about the native plants and birds, they are able to work towards protecting and rebuilding the forests to preserve the treasures of Hawaiʻi. Once the alien invaders are controlled or eliminated, the birds can reclaim some of their forest homes.

Photo by Joseph Kuhn

A Stately Goose

In the forests of Hawai'i, the native birds
are star performers. They have had to evolve
to survive in their island environment.
Let's meet a few of these stars.

The Nene, or Hawaiian Goose, is Hawai'i's state bird.
Like other geese, Nene fly in v-formation. Their
webbed feet are smaller than those of most geese
and they prefer land to water. They find grass shoots
and berries growing on the rocky lava flows, open
grasslands or even on golf courses. The Nene usually
hide their down-filled nests under low vegetation,
hoping to protect their eggs and young.

An 'Alala at home in the 'ohi'a forest.
Photo by Jack Jeffrey

Not Just Any Old Crow

The 'Alala or Hawaiian crow is one of the most critically endangered birds in the world. There are fewer than ten 'Alala left in the wild. These few birds live on ranch lands in the damp forests of the Big Island, where some landowners are working hard to preserve the birds' habitat and hopefully save the

Biologists use a puppet that resembles an adult 'Alala to feed chicks raised in captivity.
Photo by Cyndi Kuehler

remaining birds.

The 'Alala is a passerine, or perching songbird, related to many of the smaller birds of the forest. The crow is the size of a small hawk, with dark feathers the color of licorice. Its long black bill is thick and pointed, perfect for a bird with a hearty appetite. The 'Alala feeds on fruits and seeds, flowers, insects, nectar, and the flesh of dead animals.

The crows travel in family groups, flying through the treetops. They begin nesting in spring, making their nests from twigs and branches and lining them with soft plant material. The 'Alala usually lay two or three blue-green eggs speckled with brown and black. The parents become very anxious if they are disturbed on the nest. Mongoose and rats threaten the chicks and eggs of 'Alala.

Because so few 'Alala remain in the wild, many efforts are being made to save the bird from extinction. Government agencies, lawmakers, environmental

Did you know?

When many groups work together for the survival of a species or habitat, they form a Conservation Partnership. They operate as a club, holding meetings to make rules and plans to help them reach their goals. The ʻAlala Partnership includes the U.S. Fish and Wildlife Service, Kamehameha Schools Bernice Pauahi Bishop Estate, McCandless Ranch, Kealia Ranch, The Peregrine Fund, and the State of Hawaiʻi.

groups, researchers, and landowners are working together as conservation partners. The habitat of the ʻAlala is being carefully guarded. Birds are being bred in captivity and the young are returned to the wild. Now that's something to crow about!

Staying Afloat

The ʻElepaio is the guardian spirit of canoe makers. The sight of an ʻElepaio picking at a branch, searching for insects, is a warning to canoe builders that the tree is infested with bugs. No one wants a canoe with ready-made leaks!

Photo by Joseph Kuhn

Tails up, it's ʻElepaio!

Hikers walking through the wet forests on the slopes of Hawaiʻi or Kauaʻi may find themselves sharing the trail with an ʻElepaio. The bold flycatchers dart beneath the canopy or perch on the sides of tree trunks, their tails raised in proud salute. They search for insects, pecking at foliage and inspecting bark. Sometimes hikers call 'Elepaio from their forest hiding places by imitating their whistle. When an 'Elepaio sings, its song is a tuneful ele-PAI-o, sounding just like its name.

'Elepaio are common in the wet valleys and mountains on Hawai'i and Kaua'i. A few are still found on O'ahu. They collect grass, lichen, and roots of small plants to weave into nests where the female lays two or three eggs. The drab colored young remain in the nest for about two weeks after they hatch.

Adult birds vary in appearance from island to island. On Kaua'i, they are a dull brownish gray with pale bellies. In the wet areas of Hawai'i, the birds are much darker in color, and have chocolate-colored backs. Their bellies are auburn, almost red. 'Elepaio have white wing markings, tail spots and patches at the base of their tails. It is their upright tails that help birdwatchers tell them apart from the other forest birds.

A Hush of Thrush

Except for the gentle quivering of their wings, Hawai'i's native thrushes perch motionless on tree branches, or flit through the forest searching for food. Their whistled songs resemble the melodious sounds of a flute. They are descendants of birds from North and South America, and many are so critically endangered that their songs may soon disappear.

Have you ever sat at the beach watching the surfers catch the rolling waves? What if the waves disappeared? Suppose someone built a giant wall and that stretch of ocean became nothing more than a swimming pool. The surfers would search for another beach. They may have to find another island. Waves are the surfers' habitat.

If we look at what happens when we take away what is needed for a group of people to survive, we can understand what has happened to some of the birds of the forest. One thrush, the Oloma'o, became extinct on Lana'i, but continued to live on Moloka'i high in the mountains. Now it is more than ten years since anyone has seen this bashful bird.

... when the 'Oma'o sings, ... its shrill, sharp whistle could be mistaken for the whistle of a soccer referee.

The 'Oma'o, or Hawaiian Thrush, lives on the Big Island of Hawai'i. There's nothing outstanding about its dull, brown back and light gray chest feathers. Yet when the 'Oma'o sings, its series of erratic chirps and short whistles make it the most distinctive bird of the forest. Its shrill, sharp whistle could be mistaken for the whistle of a soccer referee.

'Oma'o feast on berries and insects from the native forests. They are especially fond of olapa fruit. The 'ohi'a and koa trees provide perfect nesting sites for the thrushes. Collecting vegetation such as grass, mosses and ferns from the forest, the birds build their nests in

An ʻOmaʻo feeds on
pilo berries.
Photo by
Jack Jeffrey

A nest of
Puaiohi in the
Alakaʻi Swamp.
Photo by
Jack Jeffrey

hollows of the trees.

'Oma'o are still fairly common in the higher forests and will even find food and shelter on the lava flows, or the dry alpine slopes of Mauna Loa. Occasionally, they are found farther down the mountains, as low as 1,800 feet.

On Kaua'i two critically endangered thrushes, the Puaiohi and Kama'o, make their home on the higher slopes in the 'Alaka'i Swamp. Puaiohi are sometimes called Palmer's Thrush or Small Kaua'i Thrush. They move secretively about the forest understory, hiding beneath ferns and thick vegetation, and searching for fruit and insects. Puaiohi nest in the moist mosses and lichens growing on the sides of steep gorges. For now, the numbers of Puaiohi remain steady in their remote habitats, but there are only about 300 birds left in the wild. The survival of the larger and more tuneful Kama'o is not so certain. Not one has been seen since 1989. Like the Oloma'o, this Large Kaua'i Thrush is probably extinct.

Jeepers Creepers

One small bird species, much like a finch, is believed to be the ancestor of the many species of honeycreepers native to Hawai'i. When this bird first arrived on the islands, there were few, if any, other birds living there. Gradually, over thousands of years, a whole range of new species developed.

Each species adapted to its new and changing environment. Most birds became specialized, depending

Bird Talk

Birds produce the most complicated sounds of any animals. You need only stand still and listen to the sounds of the forest to hear the many different songs and calls that the birds use to communicate. In dense forests, biologists often rely on the songs to find the birds.

From short, sharp chirps to high pitched squeals, birds use calls to warn each other of danger or draw attention to food and territory. Sometimes they communicate with each other as they feed — a conversation around the dinner table. But the long and varied songs are usually heard in mating season, when the males try to attract a mate of the same species or scare off a male rival.

Many of the forest birds have strange sounding names that are onomatopoetic. This means that their names sound like the calls the birds make. For example, the 'Akohekohe makes a sound that sounds like the creaking of a rusty old gate. (Try saying "a-ko-he-ko-he" from the back of your throat.)

Birds learn their songs from others of their species living in the same area. Learning to speak "Thrush" or "Honeycreeper" would be too difficult for even the smartest person, but we can sometimes imitate the simplest calls.

on a particular habitat for survival. When habitats were destroyed or drastically altered to make way for crops and buildings many species became extinct. Only fossils remain to show that the birds lived there.

Today, native honeycreepers include seed eaters, insect eaters and nectar eaters. Many honeycreepers are so rare that they are seldom seen, or only remain in small numbers on one island. They are critically

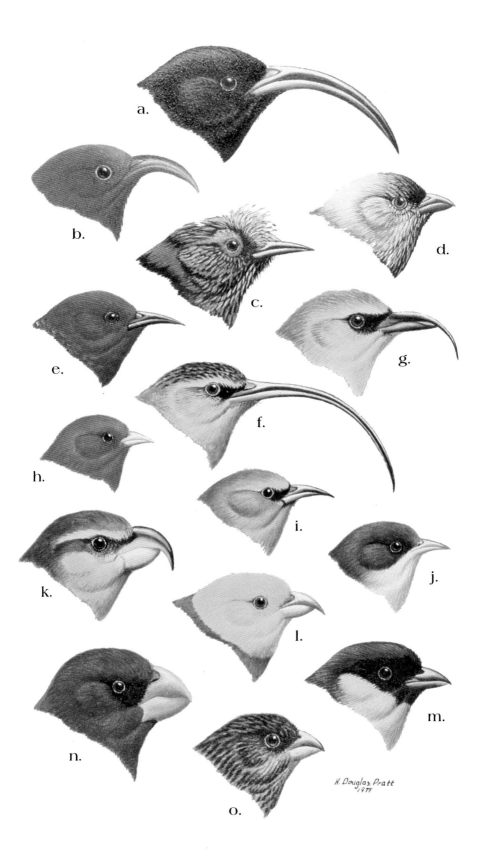

a.

b.

c.

d.

e.

g.

f.

h.

i.

k.

j.

l.

n.

m.

o.

H. Douglas Pratt
1978

endangered and some may already be extinct. That's creepy.

Fast Food

Are They Really Creepy?

When you look at a honeycreeper, you won't find the hairs standing up on the back of your neck. You won't shudder or scream. Honeycreepers get their name from the way they edge along branches and twigs, or creep among the blossoms looking for food.

When honeycreepers are hungry, they don't have to worry about cooking dinner, setting the table, or washing up when they're done. Honeycreepers have the perfect utensils for finding and eating their favorite foods. Their bills serve as forks, knives, spoons, and can openers, and they're built right into the birds. Now that's convenience.

More than in size, color or form, honeycreepers vary most in the shape of their bills. Look at the painting on the previous page, and you'll discover it's not hard to imagine what some of these birds eat.

a. Mamo

b. 'I'iwi

c. 'Akohekohe

d. Ula-Ai-Hawane

e. 'Apanane

f. Kaua'i 'Akialoa

g. 'Akiapolaau

h. Hawai'i 'Akepa

i. Hawai'i 'Amakihi

j. Kaua'i Creeper

k. Maui Parrotbill

l. 'O'u

m. Po'ouli

n. Grosbeak Finch

o. Nihoa Finch

Painting by
H. Douglas Pratt, Jr.

Kauaʻi ʻAmakihi.
Photo by Jack Jeffrey

Something in Common

The ʻAmakihi is one of the honeycreepers most often found in native forests. ʻAmakihi vary slightly from one area to the other. The yellow Common ʻAmakihi on Hawaiʻi is more colorful than its greenish yellow and brown cousins. The Kauaʻi ʻAmakihi has the longest beak and feeds mostly on insects.

ʻAmakihi feed on berries, fruit, nectar and insects. They prefer to live at high elevations, building their nests in the branches of tall trees. ʻAmakihi are star survivors in the forest.

Common 'Amakihi.
Photo by Jack Jeffrey

Islands Apart

he black-masked Hawai'i Creeper is found only at higher elevations on the Big Island, feeding on insects, and occasionally on nectar in the 'ohi'a forests. The 'Alauahio, or Maui Creeper, is still fairly common in the native forests of East Maui, where it, too, feeds on insects. On Kaua'i, the 'Akikiki, or Kaua'i Creeper is found in the 'Alaka'i Swamp, and sometimes at Koke'e State Park. Occasionally, it adds the fruits and nectars of the forest to its diet of bugs. The creepers gather mosses and small roots to build nests in trees. The 'Alauahio's nest is cone-shaped. The 'Akikiki's and Hawai'i Creeper build nests that resemble small cups.

Maui Parrotbill.
Photo by Jack Jeffrey

Bugs in the System

There are more bugs in the forest than you can count. In fact there are so many, some may have yet to be discovered. They are an important part of each ecosystem and a tasty treat for many of the birds of the forest. Nukupu'u and 'Akiapola'au have upper beaks, or mandibles, that are long and curved. Their lower mandibles are much shorter. The birds use their sharp, upper bills to tear away bark or dig in wood, as they search for spiders and insects.

Little is known about the rare Nukupu'u. They have occasionally been seen eating nectar from brightly colored forest flowers, such as lobelia. In the past ten years, the Nukupu'u has been seen less than

A male Palila feeds on mamane pods.
Photo by Jack Jeffrey

ten times.

'Akiapola'au are found only on the Big Island, where they usually feed on larvae and bugs from the 'ohi'a forests. Occasionally, they appear in Mauna Kea's mamane forests.

The Maui Parrotbill has a short, sharp bill and resembles a small parrot. It splits open bark and branches, using its tongue and upper mandible to tug out insects and larvae. Po'ouli, too, have short bills and pull moss and foliage from branches, searching for wood borers or caterpillars. A lucky Po'ouli might find a crunchy snail for supper.

Bean Birds

Yellow-hooded Palila, nick-named the "yellow-headed bean-eaters," clutch the pods of the mamane tree with their feet. They use their beaks to rip open pods and

An ʻApapane perches among the
colorful blossoms of an ʻohiʻa.
Photo by Jack Jeffrey

reach the tough young seeds inside. The endangered Palila live in the forests of Mauna Kea on the Big Island, where the seedpods are plentiful. Palila will also feed on insects, naio berries and flowers, and leaves. They build their nests in the top of the mamane trees. In order to increase the numbers of Palila, scientists must also increase the mamane forest and try to fight the avian diseases which threaten the birds.

The Big Sippers

The 'I'iwi use their long, orange beaks to slurp the nectar from 'ohi'a flowers or feed insects to their young. Young birds are mottled yellow and orange, but the adults are scarlet red and have handsome black wings and tail. Very few 'I'iwi have survived on O'ahu or Moloka'i, but they are more common in the canopy of the high forests on Maui, Kaua'i and Hawai'i.

'Akohekohe are the bossiest birds of the forest and often scare away other birds to feed.

The black-billed 'Apapane and the 'Akohekohe, or Crested Honeycreeper, also feed on the nectar of the 'ohi'a. 'Apapane eat insects and blossoms of native forests too. Sometimes they will eat from flowering trees, such as eucalyptus, which are not native to the forest.

'Akohekohe, with their dark bodies and odd tufted

crest, are the bossiest birds of the forest and easily identified by their series of noisy calls. On Maui, on the slopes of Haleakala, 'Akohekohe will often scare away other birds to feed on 'ohi'a nectar or other native plants and insects.

The 'Akepa, very near extinction on Maui but sometimes found on the higher slopes of Hawai'i, occasionally feed on 'ohi'a nectar. More often they use their cone-shaped bills to pry open the seed pods and buds in search of insects. Kaua'i 'Akepa, or 'Akeke'e, also feed in the 'ohi'a and koa forests. 'Akepa nest in the cavities of the 'ohi'a but 'Akeke'e nest in branches. The 'ohi'a are these birds' best friends.

The Legendary 'Ohi'a Plant

'Ohi'a trees come in all shapes and sizes. Their nectar-filled flowers may be shades of red, orange, yellow, or even white. The trees grow on low plains and high mountains, on rocky lava plains, and in fertile, wet soil. No wonder so many different birds search them out.

As a part of the cultural traditions of the islands, 'ohi'a has been used to make household utensils, religious images and buildings. According to legend the flower was sacred to Pele, the goddess of fire. The Hawaiian god, Ku, sometimes appeared as an 'ohi'a tree. Many parts of the plants were used in ancient remedies.

Did you know?

The crimson feathers of the 'I'iwi and 'Apapane were commonly used in feather work. Warriors' canoes carried heads of Ku, the god of war, made from feathers of the 'I'iwi .

An 'Io with nestling. Photo by Jack Jeffrey

Here, There and Everywhere

The 'Io and the Pueo are the only native birds of prey that have survived in Hawai'i.

'Io, or Hawaiian Hawks, soar proudly on the wind. They swoop to the ground, grabbing up small birds and rats with their strong talons. Deep in the forests 'Io feed on insects, too.

During the mating season, the 'Io screech loudly. They gather twigs and leaves to build their nests in trees of the forest. A female lays as many as three pale blue eggs, but usually only one chick will successfully

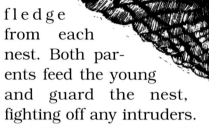

fledge
from each
nest. Both par-
ents feed the young
and guard the nest,
fighting off any intruders.

Pueo.
Illustration by
Michael Furuya

The Pueo is also known as the Hawaiian or Short-eared Owl. The Pueo has tufts of feathers that look like ears but you won't notice them from far away. Unlike most owls, Pueo do not wait until night to hunt for food. In the early morning and evening, they hover over grasslands searching for insects and rodents. Although Pueo have bigger heads and shorter necks, in flight they may be hard to tell from the 'Io. They build their nests in long grass and lay three to six white eggs. Pueo can be seen in many parts of the islands, especially on Kaua'i, Maui and Hawai'i.

Spotting Tips:

LOOK UP! Perhaps you'll be lucky enough to see an 'Io on the Big Island, soaring above the valleys or lower slopes of Hawai'i Volcanoes National Park or swooping down to grasslands and canefields near Hilo and along the Hamakua Coast.

You'll notice the v-shape in the sky. Some birds have pale chests with dark streaking. The dark brown feathers of the 'Io may appear black if you are a long way off and their gray tails are streaked with brown.

Did you know?

The Pueo, with its speckled plumage, yellow eyes, and feathered feet and legs, was worshipped by ancient Hawaiians as Kane, the most powerful of all gods.

Action Stations

n 1973 the Federal Government passed the Endangered Species Act to try and help save wildlife and plants threatened with extinction. Twenty-one of Hawai'i's rarest forest bird species were listed as endangered. Plans were made to protect the birds and their habitats. A counterattack began to repair damage caused over hundreds of years. The native birds, stars of the forest, had found allies in their fight for survival.

Saving just one species of animal is an enormous task. Now, more than twenty years after the Act was passed, scientists are seeing signs of change and hope for the future of many endangered species. There are

Top: Hawaiian students learn about the changes taking place in native forests at The Keauhou Bird Conservation Center.
Photo by L. DiSante.

Above: A Puahiohi, reared by The Peregrine Fund, feeds on a mealworm.
Photo by Jim Denny.

Above: Marla Kuhn, a biologist with The Peregrine Fund, brings endangered ʻAlala eggs from the wild. The eggs will be hatched in an incubator where they are safe from predators.
Photo by Cyndi Kuehler.

stricter laws to help protect the native species, and to stop the importation of animals and the spread of diseases from other parts of the world.

Hundreds of people are involved in the effort to save the feathered treasures of Hawai'i's forests. Environmental groups, landowners, conservationists, and biologists work together. They share their knowledge and closely observe changes in the forest.

Some conservationists destroy alien vegetation that is killing native plants, or grow native plants to help restore the forest. Others trap non-native animals and build miles of fences to keep native species safe. Scientists hatch eggs collected from nests, raise the young birds, and return them to the wild. Some landowners protect those parts of their land which are important habitats for native birds. Volunteers help, too.

Students catch insects to feed to 'Elepaio being bred in captivity.
Photo by L. DiSante

Students help plant native trees.
Photo by L. DiSante

Bringing Back the Songs

[ducation plays an important role in saving the feathered treasures of the rainforest. In classrooms, nature centers, zoos, and parks, people are learning about the rare birds of Hawaiʻi. As scientists find out more about the fragile species, they are able to work more effectively. As the Hawaiian people know more about the native birds, they are able to help preserve an important part of their cultural heritage. Students learn about native flora and fauna in school. Some volunteer in conservation programs. You, too, can help change the future of these rare birds.

Hawaiian Proverb:

If you plan for a year, plant kalo.

If you plan for ten years, plant koa

If you plan for one hundred years, teach the children.

This day-old Hawai'i 'Akepa, no larger than a jelly bean, would have a difficult time surviving in the wild without habitat management and protection.
Photo by Joseph Kuhn.

Armed for Combat

How can you help in the battle against alien invaders? Here are some ideas.

Be a Bird Nerd

Learn all that you can about Hawaiian birds. Read books, magazines and newspapers. Watch nature programs on TV. Visit museums, nature centers and parks. Search the computer for bird-friendly sites.

Tell It Like It Is

Share your knowledge with your family, friends, and neighbors. Let them know ways they can help.

Save Your Energy

Just as a car cannot run without gas, none of us can live without water. Respect and help preserve the forests that provide our water supply. Use water wisely. Bike or walk to help keep our air clean. Recycle. Help make the earth a healthier place.

Get Your Hands Dirty

Grow some native plants to help bring the plants of the forest back. Clean up water puddles that attract mosquitoes. Get rid of trash that attracts pests. Join a volunteer group and help clear the forests of alien plants.

Stop, Look, and Listen!

Take a walk in the forest. Watch for the shimmering of leaves or the sudden bending of a branch. Hear the rustling on the forest floor, the busy chirping in the tall trees, the flutter of small wings. Feel the moist air on your face. Close your eyes. You are sharing one of the most precious places on Earth.

Glossary

adapt — change to fit the environment

avian — of or about birds

canopy — the upper layer of the forest formed by the treetops

ecosystem — plants and animals interacting with each other and their environment

endangered — under threat of dying out

evolution — gradual change leading to new species

extinct — no longer in existence

feral — wild or untamed

forage — search for food

habitat — the place where an animal or plant lives

mandible — the upper or lower part of the beak

native — an original inhabitant, belonging to a particular area

passerine — a perching bird or songbird

quarantine — isolation of an animal to prevent spread of disease

specialized — adapted to a particular environment

species — individual animals that can breed with each other

understory — the lowest level of the forest above the forest floor

wallow — a muddy bog caused by trampling and rooting up plants

Treasure Hunting?

If you'd like to know more about the star performers, here's where you'll find them:

A Fund of Information

If you would like to learn more about the birds of the rainforest or become a member, contact The Peregrine Fund.

The Peregrine Fund
Keauhou Bird Conservation Center
P.O.Box 39
Volcano, HI 96785
Tel: (808) 985-7218
Fax: (808) 985-7034
e-mail: HTSU21A@prodigy.com

You can visit their website at:
http://www.peregrinefund.org

To order more copies of this book, contact The Peregrine Fund at the above address.